Katrin Unterreiner

# The Hofburg

Sights · Museums · Art treasures

With photos by
Willfried Gredler-Oxenbauer

Pichler Verlag

# THE VIENNA HOFBURG

In contrast to most residences, the Vienna Hofburg is not one unified palace complex but an asymmetrical complex that covers 240,000 m² (2,583,338 sq ft) and consists of 18 wings with over 2600 rooms, 54 staircases, 19 inner courtyards and squares and two large gardens.

From the beginning of their rule in Austria in the 13th century until the end of the monarchy in 1918, the Habsburgs lived and resided in Vienna, thus making the city the centre of European politics and history for 640 years.

Yet the Hofburg Palace was more than an imperial residence. For centuries, up to 2000 people lived and worked here. Each Habsburg ruler left behind his or her traces and not only influenced the image of the Hofburg with their respective lifestyles but also life at the Vienna court. Therefore, this book not only searches for architectural vestiges but also tries to trace daily court life based on several of the Habsburgs – above all Emperor Franz Joseph and Empress Elisabeth – and also to follow up on questions such as which wing had which function, where and when the royal family lived and how their daily schedule was planned.

This not only includes the royal family but also the royal household and the question as to where the most important facilities such as the kitchen, store cupboards and wine cellars were situated; where and how the numerous servants lived and slept; and how the organisation of the royal household was controlled.

As well as taking care of the royal family, daily challenges also included audiences, receptions, gala dinners and court balls for several thousands of people. But also traditions, which at the time of the monarchy were dearly loved by the Viennese, such as the spectacular, musically underscored sled races in the 18th century or the change of the castle guards in the inner palace courtyard which occurred until the end of the monarchy.

Even today, the Hofburg is not a museum in the classical sense, but has kept its function as an important focal point of the city, which is why various ministerial, institutional and union offices and also parts of the Vienna University are housed in many of its wings and rooms. Private apartments also contribute to keeping the former royal premises a lively complex.

**Above:** In front of the erstwhile drawbridge over the former moat of the Alte Burg are two stone heraldic lions from the 18th century. The left lion is holding the Austrian shield, the one on the right, a shield with five eagles, Lower Austria's coat of arms.
**Opposite page:** The main entrance of the Neue Hofburg on Heldenplatz.

The Prince Eugene monument on Heldenplatz.

Detail of the monument to Emperor Franz II/I in the Inner Burghof

Detail of the Palm House in the Burggarten.

**Above:** The magnificent staircase in the Neue Hofburg stretches over almost the whole length of the structure. At the centre of the complex is the so-called "Hunting plateau", which is also used for festive events.

**Below:** Emperor Franz Joseph's conference room.

Empress Elisabeth's large salon.

# ST. MICHAEL'S WING

With its large, characteristic dome and two huge fountains, St. Michael's Wing (Michaelertrakt) has represented the entrance of the Hofburg since the 19th century. St. Michael's façade, completed by Ferdinand Kirschner in 1893 based on blueprints by Josef Emanuel Fischer von Erlach, completes the Hofburg on the inner-city side and received its name from St. Michael's church. This part of the Hofburg was originally outlaid with guest apartments. The financial department and the court treasury were on the ground floor.

The decorative sculptures on the façade were supposed to represent the power and fame of the House of Habsburg. The façade is dominated by two monumental wall fountains; on the left side "Supremacy at Sea" by Rudolf Weyr and on the right Edmund von Hellmer's "Supremacy on Land". Both sides of the thoroughfare are decorated by Lorenzo Mattielli's statue series "Deeds of Hercules", which is continued in the inner Burghof (Castle Court). The gable is crowned by the allegories of wisdom, justice and power. Above the centre passageway is the Habsburg imperial family's coat of arms flanked by two trombone-playing Famae proclaiming the dynasty's worldly fame. In the middle is the Austrian shield – today's red-white-red Austrian coat of arms – on the left, the rising Habsburg lions and on the right the three diagonal Lorrainian eagles. Following the death of the last Habsburg, Charles VI, in 1740 and after his daughter and heiress Maria Theresia had married Franz Stephan of Lorraine, the dynasty was officially called Habsburg-Lorraine and also used the Lorrainian arms in the family coat of arms.

The archaeologist Friedrich Kenner put together the programme of sculptures and reliefs in the thoroughfare, a programme oriented on Roman imperial iconography. The high reliefs in the vestibule of the dome hall show *Profectio Augusti* and *Adventus Augusti*; in the niches, personified by the statues, *Pietas Augusti* and *Providentia Augusti*. In the octagonal alcove itself are the maxims of the four rulers referenced in the inscription. The maxims are each exemplified in two allegorical figures: *Constantia et fortitudine* for Charles VI, *Justitia et clementia* for Maria Theresia, *Virtute et exemplo* for Joseph II, and *Viribus Unitis* for Franz Joseph I.

During the monarchy's reign, the entrance to Emperor Franz Joseph's private living quarters was situated in the dome hall. Today this is the tour entrance to the imperial apartments, the Sisi Museum and the Hofsilber and Tafelkammer (Chamber of Court Silver and Tableware).

**Above:** With the construction of the Michaelertrakt at the end of the 19th century, the Hofburg received its representative façade facing the inner city and a trademark visible from afar with a cupola that measures 54 metres in height.
**Opposite page:** The completed Michaelertrakt gave the Hofburg official access to the Imperial Apartments. Entering through the wrought-iron door takes you to St. Michael's Dome, where the emperor disembarked from his carriage and entered his apartment. Today this is the entrance to the Imperial Apartments, the Sisi Museum and the former Chamber of Court Silver and Tableware.

**Above and opposite page:** The decorative sculptures on the attic of the Michaelertrakt showing the three sovereign's virtues – justice, wisdom and power – were created by sculptor Johann Benk.
**Below left:** Detail of the huge wall fountain "Supremacy at Sea" by Rudolf Weyr on St. Michael's façade, facing the Winter Riding School.
**Below right:** Greek myth as décor: The statue cycle "The Deeds of Hercules" by Lorenzo Mattielli (detail).

In the middle of the square, designed by architect Hans Hollein, is a part of the excavations from 1990/91, which brought remnants from various centuries to the light of day: Among them Roman houses with floor heating and wall paintings from the 2nd and 5th centuries; foundations of the old Burgtheater and remnants of the so-called *Paradeisgartl*, the Baroque garden complex from Maria Theresia's time that no longer exists.

**Above:** The golden Habsburgs coat of arms over the wrought-iron gate of the Michaelertrakt.
**Right:** View from inside St Michael's Dome to the inner city of Vienna.

# CHAMBER OF COURT SILVER

The Chamber of Court Silver (formerly known as the Chamber of Court Silver and Tableware), is the unique collection of objects that were used for the organisation of the royal household. The museum not only reflects the splendour of the imperial tableware but also provides insight into the courtly dining culture and how it was executed. The administration of the Chamber of Court Silver lay in the hands of the Master of Silverware, who first became responsible for the silver and tableware at the Viennese court in the 15th century, but also for fruit and bread. Over time, the Chamber of Court Silver became increasingly more important, and the various tasks were shared between the court kitchen, confectionery, laundry, cellars, chamber of silver and tableware, kitchen garden (grocery storeroom), wood and coal storeroom and the light room, the so-called offices, which administered the royal household.

After the fall of the monarchy in 1918, the court household was dissolved, and the imperial inventory became the property of the Austrian Republic. Part of it is still used for prestigious official state dinners, but the main part went to the exhibition collection, where today about 7000 of a total of 150,000 objects are displayed on about 1300 m² (14,000 sq ft). Among these objects are gold, silver and porcelain services as well as valuable glasses, cutlery sets and not least utensils from the court kitchen. Particularly magnificent is the famous, massive Milan Centrepiece, which was ordered when Emperor Ferdinand was crowned King of Lombardy-Venetia in the year 1838. It is the silver chamber's most comprehensive ensemble and can be extended to a length of 30 metres (100 ft) with mirrored extension leaves.

**Opposite page:** Detail of the magnificent Old French tableware made of gilded bronze. The piece was ordered in 1838 when Emperor Ferdinand was crowned King of Lombardy-Venetia in Paris.
**Below left:** A few parts of the former court table silverware are still used for state banquets.
**Below right:** Small, sweet-filled boxes with portraits of royal family members were favoured as donations at the Viennese balls, but also as mementos for guests to the court table.

The impressive Milan Centrepiece exhibits the splendour of the imperial tableware, which was additionally decorated with luxurious flower bouquets.

Most of the court's silver cutlery service was manufactured by the Viennese firm Mayerhofer & Klinkosch.

One of the most important services of the court silver chamber is the Grand Vermeil. This main work of French goldsmithery from Vermeil – fire-gilded silver – originally encompassed objects for 40 place-settings and was expanded to 140 by Viennese silversmiths around 1850.

**Above:** The Grand Vermeil service is made up of a total of 4500 parts and weighs more than a tonne.
**Below:** The gold service is one of the most magnificent porcelain services of the royal court. All the individual pieces of the 12-part dinner service are coated with polished gold and were manufactured in the Viennese porcelain factory for the Vienna Congress in 1814.

# SISI MUSEUM

Today the imperial chambers can be reached the same way as Emperor Franz Joseph also once entered them: via the imperial staircase. At the beginning of the tour through the Sisi Museum and the attached Imperial Apartments, two rooms provide information about the dynasty of the Habsburgs as well as the construction history of the Hofburg. A model gives you an overview of the whole complex.

In the front rooms is the Sisi Museum, which has existed since 2004 and focuses on the vestiges of the legendary empress. As a beautiful and all-round highly acclaimed empress, Elisabeth became a cult figure. The Sisi Museum compares the myths and the facts. At the beginning of the exhibition the focus is on the tragic assassination of the empress. Her death not only represented the end of the eventful, unhappy and often misunderstood life of a unique personality, but also decisively led to the emergence of a myth, which Elisabeth herself encouraged during her lifetime by maintaining an unconventional lifestyle. At the centre of the exhibition is Elisabeth's private life and her evolution from an easy, natural and shy girl to a disappointed, disquieted, enquiring woman. From the first day

onwards, Sisi felt uncomfortable in her new role as empress, but in the beginning still tried to fulfil expectations. But she found her royal duties difficult; representational functions and the strict court ceremonials were a burden. Because Elisabeth withdrew more and more from the public eye, she was blatantly criticised at court for her egocentricity, her disinterest in her function as empress as well as in the political and social situation of the monarchy. Her reaction was to become obsessed with beauty, her weight, athletic prowess, lyrical poetry and intensive travel. In 1898 at the age of 60 and at the end of her restless life, in which she often longed to die, Elisabeth was murdered by an Italian anarchist.

In the Sisi Museum using numerous personal objects, the empress' life is vividly depicted. On show is a reconstruction of Sisi's eve-of-the-wedding party dress, one of her few preserved summer dresses, her travel toiletry set, her water colour painting set, some of her own drawings and sketches, her travel first-aid kit, a walk-in reconstruction of her luxurious court carriage as well as the most famous portraits.

**Opposite page:** In the Sisi Museum in the Imperial Apartments the visitor can follows traces of the eccentric Empress Elisabeth, who became a legend due to her unconventional lifestyle and tragic death.

"At court": Elisabeth detested her role as Empress of Austria from the beginning. In May 1854, a few days after marrying Emperor Franz Joseph she wrote: "Oh, that I had never left the path that would have set me free ..."

**Below left:** For her train journeys through Europe Elisabeth had her own custom-made luxurious court salon carriage.
**Below right:** Sisi's first-aid kit, which accompanied her everywhere she went, included a cocaine injection, which she had prescribed by her doctors for "physical and emotional exhaustion" and "melancholy".

**Above:** Empress Elisabeth in court gala dress with the famous diamond stars in her hair, painting by Franz Xaver Winterhalter, 1865.
**Below:** In order to go down in history as a young, beautiful woman, Elisabeth allowed no more photos to be taken of her after she turned 30. The last painting she posed for is from 1879, aged 42, when she was portraited by Georg Raab to celebrate the silver anniversary of the royal couple.

**Below:** On September 9, 1898, Elisabeth spent one night in Hotel Beau Rivage in Geneva. By coincidence the Italian anarchist Luigi Luccheni heard she was staying there and lurked in front of the hotel the next day. He stabbed the 60-year-old empress with a file as she was on her way to the ship.

# IMPERIAL APARTMENTS

When Franz Joseph took the throne in 1848 at eighteen years of age, he moved into an apartment in the Leopoldine Wing. It wasn't until he married Elisabeth of Bavaria in 1854 that he decided to move his apartment to the Reichkanzleitrakt (Imperial Chancellery Wing). In those days the rooms were renovated and decorated in Neo-Rococo style, according to the prevailing taste. The walls and the furniture made of palisander and walnut were upholstered with red silk damask, whose pattern of corn ears represents fertility. The rooms were heated with ceramic tiled stoves, which could only be stoked from outside – in the passageway – in order not to bother the royal family and not to dirty the rooms. The chandeliers made from Bohemian lead crystal were originally lit with candles. It wasn't until 1891 that electricity was installed in the Hofburg.

The Imperial Apartments, which in recent years have been restored and refurbished in the most historically authentic way possible, not only give you an idea of imperial domestic culture but also of the every-day life of the royals - as monarchs as well as private and family people.

Emperor Franz Joseph always saw himself as the foremost functionary of his state, and performing his duties was of the highest priority. His work day began at half-past-four in the morning and after brief ablutions he went directly to his desk and began to work through the necessary official documents.

General audiences were held twice a week, and each of the inhabitants of the multinational monarchy consisting of 56 million was allowed to attend. The audience participants who were able to appear in uniform or their national dress waited in the audience waiting room until they were allowed to appear before the emperor, thus lending a lively and colourful hue to the regional and ethnic diversity of the multinational monarchy. Apart from the Austrian Hereditary Lands, which approximately correspond with today's federal states, these also included the empires of Hungary, Bohemia and Lombardy-Venetia as well as Moravia, Galicia and Lodomeria – parts of southern Poland and today's Ukraine – Carniola and the coastal land around Triest in today's Slovenia, Croatia and Dalmatia and Bosnia-Herzegovina.

The audiences were held in the adjoining audience room and, in general, only lasted a few minutes. Aided by an audience list, the emperor was informed of the reasons for the audience. These were usually private concerns such as appeals for support – also financial – of those in need; appeals for clemency against those who were falsely accused. They also included citizens who had entered public service and wanted to be formally introduced; those applying for titles, and subjects who wanted to deliver gratitude for receiving a title or a decoration. After the audiences, the emperor would return to his study to continue with his duties.

**Above:** Emperor Franz Joseph in gala uniform, Franz Xaver Winterhalter, 1865.
**Opposite page:** Emperor Franz Joseph's audience room, where public audiences were held twice a week.

During the audiences the emperor always stood at a standing desk. In front of him was the audience list, which exactly detailed the requests of the audience.

Mantelpiece clock in the emperor's study.

**Opposite page above:** At the stroke of 12 midday, lunch was brought into the emperor's study by the *valet de chambre*. Franz Joseph consumed the meal sitting at his desk to avoid losing precious time. The meal usually consisted of soup and roasted meat with vegetables. The sovereign would drink a glass of "Spaten beer". After lunch Franz Joseph would again return to the official documents. On the left the unfinished ones and on the right, the finished ones. The only treats the emperor allowed himself were his beloved cigars, mostly smoking the cheap Virginiers, the so-called "coachman cigars". In his later years, admonished by his doctor, he had to change to the lighter "Regalia Media".

**Below:** At nine o' clock the emperor's General-Adjutant registered for the audience. He was followed by the ministers – depicted here Foreign Minister Count Stefan Burian. Because Empress Elisabeth was usually travelling, Franz Joseph's study contained two portraits and numerous photographs of his wife. In the background his favourite portrait, Elisabeth in the morning sun by Franz Xaver Winterhalter, which shows the empress with her open hair draped across her breast.

Emperor Franz Joseph was known for his modest, almost spartan lifestyle, which was reflected in the interiors of his apartment. He refused a bathroom, which he considered a luxury, and used a simple washstand to wash in. He took his bath in a rubber tub that was brought into his bedroom and removed when he was finished.

Franz Joseph was one of the longest reigning monarchs in history. He reigned for 68 years until his death in 1916, when he died in the middle of World War I at the age of 86. Throughout his life he suffered numerous strokes of fate: the early death of his eldest daughter Sophie; the tragic suicide of his only son, Crown Prince Rudolf, who shot himself and his 30-year-old lover, Baroness Mary Vetsera, in his hunting lodge in Mayerling; the execution of his younger brother Max, who as Emperor of Mexico was court-martialled and shot in 1867 by the revolutionaries; and finally the murder of his beloved Elisabeth in the year 1898.

Franz Joseph was known as a modest and frugal monarch. When he first started service, the emperor's personal *valet de chambre*, Eugen Ketterl, was not only very surprised about the modest surroundings in which the emperor lived, but mostly about his private wardrobe, which he described as being "more than scanty, except for a hunting outfit, a questionably out-of-date set of tails and a salon coat that also belonged to the other side of history ..." Each new purchase was rejected by the emperor using the argument "That is too expensive". But when a piece of clothing was so worn that even the emperor admitted that it had to be discarded, it wasn't thrown away but kept until Christmas and was sold at a major auction; the proceeds went to the royal household's servants.

# THE EMPEROR'S COURT

Emperor Franz Joseph's court encompassed over 1000 people, who worked and partly also lived in the Hofburg. The top court officials were the Lord Steward (*Obersthofmeister*), the Grand Chamberlain (*Oberstkämmerer*), the Grand Marshal of the Household (*Obersthofmarschall*) and the Master of the Stables (*Oberststallmeister*).

The Lord Steward was the first dignitary of the court and was responsible for all representational and ceremonial tasks. He was also the first and highest court clerk, in charge of the management, supervision and control of all the court employees. He was the director of all court personnel and supervised service operations in all areas of court keeping, except for the valets, the chambers and the legal chambers. He had several departments under his command – among them the court ceremonies department, the court planning and construction department, the financial department or the court treasury (which paid the pensions to former court employees, their widows and children); the court doctors, pharmacy, kitchen and laundry. The Grand Chamberlain was originally in charge of the chambers and rooms. His job included the surveillance of

the emperor's apartments, wardrobe and furniture but also of all the art objects. Over time, this position also came to entail the administration of the royal collections.

The *Hofmarschallamt* (offices for the court household) was responsible for court legal matters. The Master of the Stables was responsible for the stables, the tack and harness rooms and armoury as well as the corrals.

In addition, the *leibgarde* (life guard belonging to the imperial guard) also constituted a large part of the court. The emperor was surrounded by five life guards in Vienna: the Imperial and Royal First Arcièren Life Guard, the Hungarian Noble Life Guard, the Imperial and Royal *Trabanten* Life Guard, the Imperial and Royal Life Guard *Reiter Eskadron* and the Imperial and Royal Life Guard Infantry Company. In addition to these was the military court of the emperor, which consisted of the General Adjutant and Flügel-Adjutant (*aide-de-camp*) as well as the military and cabinet office (*Kabinettskanzlei*). Other so-called court positions included the Master of the Kitchen, Master of the Silver, Master of the Tablecloth, Master of the Hunt and the Master of Ceremonies.

The empress' dressing and exercise room. To stay slim Elisabeth did sport every day: daily gymnastics with exercises on the wall bars and rings, which hang from the door frame between the dressing room and Large Salon. She preferred riding above all, but also fencing, swimming and hiking.

Adjoining the emperor's apartment in the Amalienburg were Elisabeth's quarters. Elisabeth was considered one of the most beautiful women of her time, and she was also aware of this. From the charming but shy girl, a self-confident woman developed, who recognised the power of beauty and who also knew how to get what she wanted. Elisabeth's beauty care, which took on almost cult status, filled a large part of her day. Elisabeth was particularly proud of her thick, knee-length hair, which was brushed for two to three hours a day in her salon. Elisabeth used her daily hairdressing time to learn languages, and her Greek reader Constantin Christomanos described the almost cult-like process of the hairdressing in his memoirs.

*"The hairdressing always takes about two hours", she said, "And while I'm so busy with my hair, my mind is inert. I am afraid it leaves me through the strands of my hair straight into my hairdresser's fingers. That is why my head hurts so much ..."*

Part of the empress' beauty care was also keeping trim, which actually didn't coincide with the beauty ideal at the time: a preference for rounder, more opulent women. Elisabeth was 172 cm (5"6') tall and weighed between 48 and 50 kilos (110 lbs). She had a 51 cm (20 in) waist – however we shouldn't forget that women at the time wore corsets from a very young age.

Empress Elisabeth was the first member of the imperial family to have her own bathroom installed in 1876. Her bathtub made from galvanised sheet copper is still maintained today. The main problem with the tub was the running water connection. At this time the first toilets – usually built in doorway passages – were also in use. But at court up until then, only chamber pots, which were moved in and out of the rooms, had been in use.

# COURT DINNERS

Taking place every night at 6 o'clock were the family dinners, to which the family members currently residing in Vienna were invited. Even these dinners within the closest family circles were strictly ceremonial. A meal usually consisted of nine to 12 courses and lasted about 45 minutes. The emperor always sat at the centre of the table; opposite him the empress or the next archduchess in line. Next to her was the respective guest of honour followed by the other guests according to their social ranking. Conversation was only allowed with the respective neighbour; speaking across the table was frowned upon.

The emperor was served at the same time as the guests and as soon as he was finished eating and had put down his cutlery, the meal came to an end and the dishes were removed. It became a legend that one remained hungry at court meals because Franz Joseph ate so fast, but in reality the emperor always waited for his guests to finish eating before putting down his cutlery. Following the meal, the men would retire to the smoking salon with their cigars as it was considered impolite to smoke in front of women. The women withdrew to their own salons. As a rule the emperor went to bed directly afterwards, at about nine o'clock.

**Right and below:** The court tables were decorated with gilded tableware filled with confectionery and flower arrangements – which had to be odourless.
**Opposite page:** The empress' Large Salon in which she also took breakfast with the emperor.

# INNER BURGHOF

Each wing of the inner Burghof (inner Castle Court) was built in a different century. The core of the oldest part of the Hofburg, the Alte Burg (Old Palace) in the south-eastern corner of the square, dates back to the 13th century. Opposite the Alte Burg, the Amalienburg was built in the 16th century and not connected to the medieval castle. In the 17th century Emperor Leopold had both buildings joined by the Leopoldine Wing in the south. It wasn't until the 18th century that the square was closed off with the Imperial Chancellery Wing (Reichskanzleitrakt).

The inner Burghof of today was designed as tournament and fairgrounds. In the Baroque period, numerous magnificent public festivities of the royal house took place here, drawing huge crowds. In summer, spectacular opera performances with detailed staging, backdrops and effects were hosted in the courtyard, like, for example, in July 1668, the performance of the Italian opera by Marc Antonio *Cesti Il pomo d'oro* (*The Golden Apple*). The pompous show was held over two consecutive days, involving 1000 singers, dancers, musicians and stage technicians, and was originally conceived for the wedding of Emperor Leopold I to the Spanish Infanta Margarita Teresa the year before. In the long winter months on the other hand, sled races were among the favoured amusements. During the so-called *Schlitttagen*, 'sledding days', accompanied by squires, runners and footmen, the royal family and selected members of the aristocracy took long processions to the most important squares in the city. Here they performed "carrousels" either in circles or slalom-like in lines. The appropriate musical accompaniment was provided by court timpanists and trumpeters who were pulled along on their own large sled.

View from St. Michael's dome into the Inner Burghof.

**Above:** A horse ballet performed on the occasion of the marriage between Emperor Leopold I and the Spanish Infanta Margarita Teresa on January 24, 1667, in the Inner Burghof. The emperor himself also took part in it. Etching by J. Ossenbeeck after Nicolaus van Hay.

**Below:** The monument to Emperor Franz II/I by Pompeo Marchesi stands in the centre of the Inner Burghof. Cast in the Manfredini foundry in Milan, it took 33 days, 16 oxen and 18 horses to transport the monument form Milan to Vienna. The four statues surrounding it symbolise faith, power, peace and justice. The monument carries the emperor's motto *Amorem meum populis meis* – "My love is for my peoples".

# AMALIENBURG

The Amalienburg, the construction of which was begun in 1575 and then finished in 1611 by Pietro Ferabosco, was originally a free-standing complex and not connected to the Alte Burg. The Renaissance structure built for Archduke Ernst, the younger brother of Emperor Rudolf II, first received its name in the 18th century when Empress Amalie, widow of Joseph I, lived here between 1711 and 1742. The plain façade with its broad rusticated blockwork is crowned by a tower with an early Baroque spire and a little horse as a weather vane. Additionally, the tower has an astronomical clock that shows the phases of the moon; beneath it is a sun dial.

In the second half of the 19th century Empress Elisabeth's living quarters were situated on the first floor along the palace square. After her death in 1898 until the fall of the monarchy, her quarters remained untouched.

In the rear part of the Amalienburg near Ballhausplatz the last Austrian emperor – Charles I – had his offices between 1916 and 1918. As well as the museum-like Imperial Apartments, the Amalienburg houses the offices of the Federal Chancellery and various ministries. During Empress Elisabeth's time, her eldest daughter Gisela lived on the mezzanine before she married Leopold of Bavaria and moved to Munich. Likewise on the mezzanine, the court telegraph offices were housed at one time; and on the first floor, the offices for the Stables and Mews.

At the rear, the Amalienburg was once connected to the royal infirmary via a buttress across Schauflergasse. It was disconnected in 1903.

The Amalienburg, where Empress Elisabeth's private apartments were situated.

# THE PALACE GUARD

The Imperial and Royal Life Guard Infantry Company consisted of the so-called *Hofburgwache* (palace guard). The guardsmen, colloquially referred to as *"Burggendarmen"* (palace police), were not only posted at the Hofburg in front of the Schweizertor (Swiss Gate), next to which on the ground floor their offices where situated, but also in Schönbrunn and the court theatres and museums. The palace guards' offices were on the ground floor of the Leopoldine Wing.

In front of the guardroom stood the so-called buzz post, which the sentry had to notify with a loud, shrill call of "Present arms!" when a court party was nearing. Three calls were made if it was the emperor or empress; for archdukes and archduchesses only one. The guard then had to shoulder arms accompanied by a drum roll.

The guard changed every day at noon, during which the palace police marched slowly from the grounds to the barracks accompanied by the *Grenadiermarsch*. The most splendid and most loved spectacle, however, was the daily change of the main guard, which alternated with the regiments of the Vienna garrison. The palace guard posts were manned 24 hours a day; the stations were spread throughout the passages and staircases of the palace and the guard changed every few hours. While the change of guard took place, starting around 1 p.m., the orchestra played in the courtyard.

Emperor Franz Joseph passing the palace guard at the Swiss Gate in his carriage.

A favourite concert was the one given for the infantry regiment "Hoch- und Deutschmeister" No. 4, which marched in with its kapellmeister Carl Michael Ziehrer, who was also much loved by the Viennese for his waltzes and operetta compositions.

At about 2 p.m. the music and the relieved guard marched back to the barracks.

**Below:** The change of guard was a spectacle eagerly attended by the Viennese.

*Fahnenübergabe der „Burgmusik" am Franzensplatz.*     *Wien 1*

# LEOPOLDINE WING

Between 1660 and 1667, supervised by Martino and Domenico Carlone, Philiberto Luchese erected a connecting building between the Alte Burg and the Amalienburg for Emporer Leopold. In his day, Emperor Ferdinand I (1503–1564) had had the so-called *Kinderstöckl* integrated into the Amalienburg – a children's wing that adjoined the Alte Burg. It was constructed for his 13 children, who could not be adequately accommodated in the Alte Burg.

Shortly after this first version of the Leopoldine Wing was completed, however, it was severely damaged during a large fire. It was reconstructed by Pietro Tencala in early Baroque style between 1668 and 1681. Without any accentuations, the façade stretches over 29 arbours, whereby its front side distinguishes itself from the Burghof with a complete renunciation of any façade structure and was deliberately adapted to the façade of the Schweizertrakt. Thus, the window frames are shaped like those of the Alte Burg, in the form of flint and fire-steels, the symbols of the Order of the Golden Fleece, as the only element of embellishment. Maria Theresia and her husband Emperor Franz Stephan had their living quarters and reception rooms in the Leopoldine Wing. The Rococo furnishings and interior from their era around 1750 are still preserved.

The state rooms in the Inner Burghof remained empty after Maria Theresia's death; those at Heldenplatz were inhabited by Joseph II and then, lastly, by Emperor Franz Joseph and Empress Elisabeth shortly after their wedding. Following this, the rooms were used as guest apartments. Since 1946, the wing has housed the offices of the Austrian president and also his residence. The second floor, which also belongs to the federal offices, was inhabited by Franz Joseph's parents, Franz Karl and Sophie. The top floor is where the servants originally lived; today this floor consists of residential flats.

The four-storey cellar of the Leopoldine Wing served as the Hofburg's wine cellar. Drinking water and bread were stored here until water pipes were laid in the mid 19th century.

**Right:** Maria Theresia reigned over the Habsburg Empire from 1740 to 1780 as Austrian Archduchess and Queen of Bohemia and Hungary. Her husband Franz Stephan of Lorraine became Emperor of the Holy Roman Empire in 1745. In the same year Martin van Meytens captured Maria Theresia as Hungarian queen.

**Above:** Following her death, Empress Maria Theresia's living quarters were left untouched and were used as a representative apartment. In her bedroom, the so-called "Rich bedroom", was her bed of state, which today is in Schönbrunn Palace. That Franz Joseph's children sometimes crept in here to play was documented in the diary entry of his youngest daughter Marie Valerie in 1882: "The company of children. First we played blind man's bluff and then hide-and-seek! We ran about everywhere [...] then I jumped on Maria Theresia's bed, and oh! It cracked!!!"

**Opposite page:** View from Heldenplatz onto the Leopoldine Wing.

**Below:** The Leopoldine Wing seen from Outer Burgplatz, today the Heldenplatz. Etching by Salomon Kleiner from 1725.

# FEDERAL CHANCELLERY

At the western end of the Leopoldine Wing going towards Ballhausplatz, the Bellaria, is the entrance to the Federal Chancellery offices. Since 1946, the office of the Austrian Federal President has been situated in the Maria-Theresia state rooms.

At the western end is a chapel that even few Viennese know about, but which is not open for public access and only accessible to the president's official guests. In a narrow antechamber of the presidential offices there is an inconspicuous door to what looks like a cabinet. Opening it, one looks down into a small church that is several storeys high. It is built on the inside of the Leopoldine Wing. The "cabinet door" provides access to the oratory from which Maria Theresia was able to hear the mass without leaving her apartment. The Josephkappelle's four upper windows, which look out to Heldenplatz, are only a little higher than the rest of the long wing so that an outsider has no idea as to what lies behind them. The wall frescoes are by Franz Anton Maubertsch; the ceiling painting is by Vinzenz Fischer, designed by Nicolaus Pacassis from the year 1772.

**Left:** The interior of the Blue Bedroom, the so-called "Large Guest Apartment", which was situated in the Leopoldine Wing near the Heldenplatz, probably originates from Empress Elisabeth's time. Her apartment was located here for three years after she married, before she moved to the Amalienburg. Following this, the rooms were reserved for guests.

**Right:** The Mirror Hall was originally used as a meeting room at big parties for the members of the royal family. In contrast to most of the other chambers, this one does not have a tiled stove but an open fire place. In 1955, shortly after the signing of the Austrian State Treaty that ended the occupation of the allies, the room was used as a venue for a gala breakfast. Participants included the foreign ministers from the four signing states, who were guests of the then president Theodor Körner.

**Opposite page:** The entrance to the presidential offices is at the western part of the Leopoldine Wing, where Maria Theresia had a ramp built – the Bellaria – so that her carriage could take her directly from the castle bastion to her quarters on the first floor.

The four-storey cellar of the Leopoldine Wing was the location of the court's wine cellar. Following its auction in 1918, plaster models found their way into storage there – sculpture designs of the Ringstrasse buildings created by important sculptors and architects of historism.

**Below left:** The walled-in wine barrel that holds 73,000 litres held the wine of the various court vineyards. The new deliveries were filled from above and the mixture was then poured out below. It is said that during World War II Russian soldiers died here – apparently they opened the barrel and died in the ensuing flood of wine.

**Below right:** Viennese court wine came from the imperial vineyards of the Austro-Hungarian monarchy as well as from well-known vineyards throughout Europe. During Franz Joseph's time chablis, Rhein wein and Bordeaux were the favoured wines; also sherry, Madeira, Tokay, Lacrima Christi, various liqueurs – and Champagne.

A hidden miniature world of monuments, fountains and Ringstrasse-palace embellishments: the so-called "plaster depot" in the Leopoldine Wing's cellar.

In what used to be the servants' quarters in the uppermost floor of the individual wings of the Hofburg are now around 60 private apartments. "Hofburg Vienna" may sound alluring as an address, but the flats are very low and only reachable via countless stairs and long corridors.

# IMPERIAL CHANCELLERY WING

It wasn't until the successful defeat of the Ottomans during the second Turkish occupation of the city in 1683 and the victorious course of the Turkish wars that the prerequisites were fulfilled to make the Hofburg a representative residence of the powerful ruling house. Up to then it had been regarded as a fortification rather than an imperial palace.

Opposite the Leopoldine Wing up until the beginning of the 18th century stood an unadorned, two-storey chancellery wing that bordered the Inner Burghof at the city end. It was connected to the Schweizerhof by a simple gate. Temporary triumph portals were erected on special occasions. With the remodelling of the Imperial Chancellery Wing, Emperor Charles VI (1711–1740) went about extending the Hofburg in Baroque style, but plans for a unified overall concept were abandoned due to unaffordable costs.

This complex, the construction of which was begun by Johann Lukas von Hildebrandt in 1723 at Schauflergasse and then completed by Josef Emanuel Fischer von Erlach at the Inner Burgplatz, encompasses several courtyards – the Marschallhof, Kaiserhof and Batthanyihof. It exhibits two different façade concepts. While Hildebrandt's façade is more conservatively designed, Fischer's at the Burgplatz end is the most exemplary of the Hofburg.

The central risalit with the Kaisertor is crowned by Emperor Charles VI's coat of arms, which shows the coat of arms of the houses Austria and Castile. Above it rises the imperial crown, surrounded by personified ruling virtues and trophies. The side risalites are decorated with an atlas and a Roman eagle, the symbol of world supremacy. The four sculpture groups of the side portals of the Burgplatz were created by Lorenzo Mattielli: Hercules and the Cretan bull, Hercules and the Nemean Lion on the north-western portal; Hercules and Busiris and Hercules, and Antaeus on the south-eastern portal. The god effigies are related to this group of figures on the Hermes pilasters over the entrance arcade, from right to left, Mars, Neptune, Janus and Zeus.

The Imperial Chancellery Wing (Reichskanzleitrakt) orginally housed the chancellery – the administrative body of the Holy Roman Empire – as well as numerous court chancelleries: the police and legal authorities, the imperial archives, also those of house (from 1806), court and state archives (until 1902), and the most important and largest of all court administrations, the supreme offices of the court (*Obersthofmeisteramt*) and the ceremonies department.

Following the dissolution of the Holy Roman Empire in the year 1806, a part of the chancellery offices were remodelled into imperial apartments, which were then occupied by Emperor Franz Joseph.

**Above:** The coat of arms of Emperor Charles VI shows the arms of the house of Austria and Castile, for Charles grew up in Spain, which back then still belonged to the Habsburgs' world empire. After the Spanish War of Succession the kingdom of Spain and its rich colonies in South America fell to the Bourbons. Charles never wanted to accept this loss and also used the insignias of the Spanish royalty during his reign.
**Opposite page:** View from the Emperor Franz II/I monument over the Imperial Chancellery Wing.

The decorated sculpture of the Imperial Chancellery Wing is by Lorenzo Mattielli and portrays the deeds of Hercules.

# OLD FORTRESS

The oldest part of the Hofburg is on the south-eastern side of the Inner Burghof: the Old Fortress (Alte Burg), which dates back to the Bohemian King Ottokar II Premysl (1253 1278), who, after the dissolution of the first Austrian dynasty – the Babenbergs – occasionally resided in Vienna in the year 1246.

The castle, which at the time had four towers and strengthened the city's fortification, represents the historical core of the Vienna Hofburg, today called the Schweizertrakt (Swiss Wing).

In 1273, following his ascension to the Roman-German throne, Rudolf I von Habsburg conquered Ottokar Premysl in the battle of Dürnkrut and Jedenspeigen in 1278 and enfeoffed Austria to his sons Albrecht I and Rudolf II. Thus the rule of the Habsburgs in Austria began, lasting until the end of the monarchy in 1918, and would decisively influence Vienna as the *Residenzstadt* (residential city) of the dynasty.

Remains of the former moat still exist in front of the Schweizertor which leads into the Alte Burg; reminiscent of the medieval castle, right and left of the gate are balls that were used to roll the drawbridge. While three of the four towers were soon broken off, the Widmertor remained in one piece up until the Baroque period. Parts of the medieval fort are still visible in the passageway to Heldenplatz.

The Hofburg would maintain its well-fortified character for a long time – not only was it close to the medieval fort, it was also part of the weir system. In any case, at the time, contemporaries were not impressed by the image of the residence. According to Merian's topography from 1649, the imperial palace wasn't "that magnificently built, and is very narrow for such a powerful and mighty sovereign". Up until the second Turkish occupation in 1683, the Hofburg's usefulness and ability to provide protection was the fundamental idea behind its architectural foundations.

In 1515 the Conference of Princes took place in the Burg. Negotiations laid the foundation for Austria's rise as a major power. Emperor Maximilian, married to Maria of Burgundy, one of Europe's wealthiest heiresses, had already married off his children to the heirs of Spain in 1496, and was negotiating with Wladislaw II, the Jagielon King of Hungary and Bohemia, about marrying off his grandson. In a ceremonious double wedding his grandson Ferdinand finally married Wladislaw's daughter Anna, while his granddaughter Maria married Wladislaw's son, King Ludwig of Hungary. Thus the Habsburgs secured themselves the Hungarian and Bohemian crowns until the end of the monarchy. This very clever marriage policy of the Habsburgs went down in history with the famous quote: *Bella gerant alii, tu, felix Austria nube!* "Other lands may wage war, but thou, oh happy Austria, marry".

**Above:** The coat of arms panel on the façade of Alte Burg used to be at the entrance of the Hofburg's former Lustgarten, which no longer exists. In the 18th century the panel was moved here.

FERDINAN DVS ROM
GERMAN HVNGAR
BOEM ZC REX INFA
HISP ARC HI AVSTR
DVX BVR GVND ZC
ANNO M D LII

# SWISS GATE

Designed by Pietro Ferabosco in 1551, the Swiss Gate (Schweizertor) is one of the most important Renaissance monuments in Vienna. The lintel was embellished with Renaissance motifs of which only the flintstone and fire-steel – the symbols of the Order of the Golden Fleece – are identifiable today. The inscription names the emperor-to-be Ferdinand I by his official titles as the Roman-German King, King of Hungary and Bohemia, Spanish Infant, Austrian Archduke and Count of Burgundy. Lining the coat of arms is the chain from the Order of the Golden Fleece; it shows the one-headed eagle, as Ferdinand was not yet emperor at this time.

In the area where the drawbridge was once lowered over the moat, are two stone lions that date back to the 18th century. The one on the left is holding the Austrian shield in his paws, while the one of the right is holding a shield with five eagles – today Lower Austria's coat of arms. The vaulted gate passageway is decorated with ceiling frescoes from 1553, which show the coat of arms of the then Austrian constituencies: the Austrian escutcheon – Austria's coat of arms – accompanied by the arms of Styria, Carniola, Carinthia and Austria above the Enns. On the base of the inner archway Emperor Leopold I personally carved Emperor Maximilian II's motto in 1660: *Si deus pro nobis quis contra nos* – When god is with us, who is against us?

**Opposite page:** The passageway to the Schweizerhof is decorated by the Renaissance portal by Pietro Ferabosco from 1551. Remnants of the original medieval palace complex have been maintained: the balls from the drawbridge chains are preserved in the upper corners of the gate arches.
**Above right:** The rendering of the Austrian coat of arms in the Schweizertor passageway dates back to 1553.
**Below right:** The escutcheon carries the five-eagle coat of arms, the coat of arms of Lower Austria. Originally the five eagles symbolised the entirety of the Habsburg possessions in the eastern alpine region, the dukedoms above and below the Enns, Styria, Carinthia, Carniola and the Windic Mark.

# SWISS WING AND HOFBURGKAPELLE

Since Maria Theresia's era, when the Swiss Guard stood guard at the Hofburg entrance, the Alte Burg has been referred to as the Schweizertrakt (Swiss Wing). Its core structure dating back to the 13th century kept its original form, an almost square, four-winged complex, except its towers that were removed by 1753. Today's façade in Renaissance style dates back to renovations done in the 1550s. In a niche left of the Schweizertor is a well, which delivered drinking water to the palace inhabitants throughout the centuries. The basin of the well has a double eagle carved into it, the only memory to Emperor Charles V in Vienna, who actually never stayed in the city.

On the right hand side is the staircase to the chapel, which in its current form dates back to 1447 to 1449, when emperor-or-to-be Frederick III commissioned the renovations and extensions of the already existing chapel. Its medieval origins are largely hidden behind the 18th century façade, which was designed by Jean Nicolas Jadot de Ville-Issey.

In the adjoining chapel, which was once the southern part of the moat and was filled in the 18th century, a part of the Gothic apse projects. The chapel with its Baroque interior is one of the most traditional venues for church music in Vienna.

The Vienna Hofmusikkapelle was reorganised by Maximilian I in 1498 and is thus the oldest, still upheld musical institution in Europe. Members of the orchestra belong to the Vienna Philharmonic; the choir consists of Vienna Sängerknaben. Each day at 9:15 a.m. a mass is held, for which tickets are necessary. However the mass is broadcast in the surrounding public rooms.

About 100 Sängerknaben, who live in the Augarten palace, are divided into four choirs. They share the duties of tours, concerts and singing in the Hofburg.

**Above:** The Sängerknaben have been singing Sunday mass in the Hofburgkapelle since 1498.
**Left:** The so-called *Botschafterstiege* (Ambassadors' Staricase) in the Schweizerhof, via which, dating back to Emperor Charles VI, ambassadors and foreign state envoys reached the ceremonial rooms for receptions. This part now belongs to the congress centre and is only open for special events

# COURT KITCHEN

The entrance to the court kitchen, on the ground floor of the Schweizertrakt, was once underneath the Hofburgkapelle. Due to the high fire risk and also because of the kitchen's odours, the kitchen rooms were deliberately placed far away from the dining rooms. To take the dishes to the table still warm, the food was transported to the preparation rooms of the dining rooms in portable boxes that were heated with coal. The court kitchen consisted of several parts: the large kitchen with spits for roasting, the cold kitchen for cold platters and patés, the salad kitchen and the desert kitchen for noodles, *Fleckerln* (pasta bakes), *Schmarren* (caramelized pancakes), strudels, and cakes. For smaller meals the royal family also had "separate kitchens", which were directly inside the apartments. The court confectionery in the Leopoldine Wing made coffee, tea, hot chocolate jam, fruit juices, ice cream and sorbets. In the passage to the chapel courtyard, the kitchen garden steps are a reminder of the large pantries and storerooms that used to be situated here, and which stored food for around 2000 servants.

**Above:** Copper baking forms from the court kitchen.
**Below:** The court kitchen's party kitchen with large and small spits.

**Above:** Huge loads – everything from building material to furniture – were pulled up to the attic using cables, here in the Batthyanyhof, and then taken to their destination.
**Below left:** Even today, the undiscovered can be discovered in the Hofburg. This includes the house altar embedded in the wall. The altar's history is still a mystery.
**Below right:** The attic of the Imperial Chancellery Wing.

# TREASURY

Today in what used to be part of the court kitchen is the Treasury (Schatzkammer), which holds Austria's most important historical treasures. The Vienna Treasury collection not only includes the Austrian imperial crown but also that of the Holy Roman Empire as well as remaining imperial regalia, including coronation apparel, among others the *globus cruciger*, the imperial Book of Gospels, the ceremonial sword and the so-called sabre of Charles the Great. The legendary agate bowl and the *Ainkhürn* are also exhibited here. The attached Ecclesiastical Treasury exhibits precious embroidered vestments from the Middle Ages and valuable monstrances.

The imperial crown, dating back to the second half of the 10th century, was the "crown of all crowns", because its meaning via the complex numbers and symbolism outshone all the other crowns. Its octagonal form refers back to the heavenly Jerusalem; the enamel representations of David, Hezekiah, Salomon and the Maiestas Domini on the plates and the inscriptions contain programmatic predicates about governance as well as the virtues of the emperor. The cross stands for the meaning of Christian belief. The inscription written in pearls on the clip (CHONRADVS DEI GRATIA ROMANORV[M] IMPERATOR AVG[VSTVS]) represents the self-confidence of the medieval rulers endowed with the divine right of kings.

As early as 1804, two years before the Holy Roman Empire was dissolved, Emperor Franz proclaimed Austria an empire as a reaction to Napoleon's proclaiming the First French Empire. In contrast to the Holy Roman Empire, the Austrian imperial line was inherited through the male family line. The imperial crown selected was that of Rudolf II from the 16th century.

**Opposite page:** Emperor Franz as Austrian emperor, painting by Friedrich Amerling.

**Above left:** The royal Bohemian elector regalia. The King of Bohemia was also an elector and thus one of the seven prince-electors whom the emperor of the Holy Roman Empire had chosen.
**Below left:** The cradle of the King of Rome – of Napoleon's son and the Austrian archduchess Marie Louise, who married the French emperor in 1810.

Exhibited in the centre of the second room of the Treasury are the insignias of the Austrian Empire; on the left is the tabard for the herald Emperor Franz I Stephan of Lorraine. In the background is the portrait of his father-in-law, Emperor Charles VI, whose daughter Maria Theresia married Franz Stephan in 1736.

# THE HOLY ROMAN EMPIRE

The Holy Roman Empire was founded on Christmas Eve in the year 800 when the Franconian King Charles the Great was crowned emperor by Pope Leo III in Aachen. The Holy Roman Empire – the sobriquet the "German nation" was first used in the 16th century – was founded by Charles as a supranational empire. Its name derives from the entitlement of the medieval ruler to carry on the tradition of the antique Roman Empire and to legitimise the empire as God's holy will in the Christian sense.

The Holy Roman Empire was an electoral kingdom. The emperor was elected Roman-German King of Bohemia by the seven *Kurfürsten* (prince-electors) named in the Golden Bull – three clerical, the archbishops of Mainz, Cologne and Treves, and four secular, the King of Bohemia, the Margrave of Brandenburg, the Count Palatine of Rhein and the Duke of Saxony. He was then crowned emperor by the pope. The Holy Roman Empire existed up until the year 1806, when it was dissolved by Emperor Franz II who was under the pressure of Napoleon's claim to power and the founding of the *Rheinbund*.

**Right:** The *globus cruciger* as the symbol of the ruling authority dates back to the predecessors of antiquity. Even back then the orb was seen as an image of the earth, the cosmos and symbol of world supremacy. Adding the cross in Early Christian times, the orb became a symbol of Christianity and thus came to stand for the rule of Christ over the world as it was known.

**Above:** Its function as a biblical legal symbol gave the sceptre particular weight as a symbol of rule. The imperial sword from 1220 was a symbol of spiritual and secular entitlement to rule, thus symbolizing the emperor's claim to leadership.

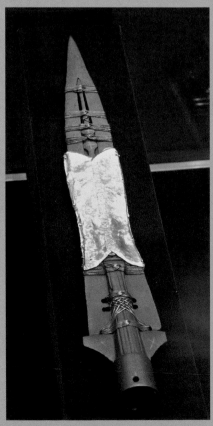

**Right:** The Holy Lance, for a long time the most distinguished imperial reliquary, symbolised dominance and reliquary at the same time due to an iron pin that is embedded in its blade. This, according to lore, dates back to Christ's Cross. For this reason the Carolingian lance from the 8th century was surety for the divine protection of the German kings and emperor of the Holy Roman Empire.

The Coronation Mantle is the centrepiece of the coronation regalia. The Arabic-Norman handiwork dates back to the years 1133/34 and was produced in the royal workshop in Palermo. The silk mantle was worn at coronations from the time of Friedrich II's coronation in 1220 to the dissolution of the Holy Roman Empire. It is embroidered with gold and over 100,000 pearls and enamel plaques. At its centre is a stylised palm tree representing the tree of life; right and left of it, a symbol of imperial power, the lion triumphs over a camel.

According to legend, the Carolingian St. Stephen's purse contained earth that was soaked in the blood of the stoned St. Stephen, thus representing a particular reliquary. It received its name from old sacks called "pilgrim bags".

The Imperial Cross from 1024/1025 also had several functions and was not only a symbol of power but also a reliquary. Its shaft has room to store the Particle of the Cross and the Holy Lance.

# COLUMN STAIRCASE AND CHAPEL COURTYARD

In the left corner of the Schweizertrakt was once the entrance to Crown Prince Rudolf's apartment, which was on the second floor towards the Heldenplatz, and is now home to the Federal Office for the Protection of Monuments. On the first floor is the Palace Administration Office, which is responsible for the administration of the huge complex and also other former imperial residences. A passageway leads to a small chapel courtyard where the gothic apse of the Hofburgkapelle built in the 16th century can be admired. A connecting passage leads to the Burggarten.

**Right:** The column staircase was once the entrance to the apartment of Crown Prince Rudolf. Here now on the first floor is the palace administration office and on the second, the Federal Office for the Protection of Monuments.
**Below:** With the apse of the Hofburgkapelle in the small chapel courtyard, remnants of the Gothic chapel can be admired.

# BURGGARTEN

After the French occupying forces destroyed the castle bastions in 1809 and the exploded fort was removed, the imperial garden complex was built, which remained the royal family's private garden until the end of the monarchy. At the northern end of is the palm house, a Jugendstil glass house built between 1901 and 1905 by Friedrich Ohmann, and which today houses a café. Hundreds of free-flying, exotic butterflies live in the butterfly house next door in a tropical miniature rain forest that is kept at 26 °C and a humidity level of 80 % in almost natural conditions. A waterfall, small ponds and bridges create a scenic backdrop in front of which the beauty of the butterflies unfolds. One of them is the large, colourful Atlas moth with its striking patterns and a wingspan of up to 30 cm. Visual aids provide information about the insects and an overview of the life cycle of a butterfly. In the so-called "pupal box" you can observe the butterflies as they hatch.

On the western side of the Neue Burg is a monument dedicated to Franz Stephan of Lorraine; in the southern corner, one dedicated to Emperor Franz Joseph. The monument presents a metal copy of the one created by Johannes Benk for the infantry cadet school, which was temporarily installed in the Wiener Neustadt municipal park and was to be scrapped in 1938. On 18 August 1957, the emperor's birthday, the monument was finally unveiled in the Burggarten.

The monument to Wolfgang Amadeus Mozart created by Viktor Tilgner in 1896 originally stood on what today is Albertinaplatz, in front of the present-day Café Mozart. Following the bombing from 12 March 1945, the monument was moved from its original location and was finally placed in the Burggarten in June 1953. On the front side's bas-relief are the invitations and the appearance of the stony guest from the opera Don Giovanni; on the rear side, the six-year-old composer at the piano, his father Leopold with violin and his sister Nannerl singing.

In 1819 Emperor Franz commissioned the architects Ludwig von Remy and Franz Antoine to design a private garden complex in place of the city walls that had been destroyed by French troops during their withdrawal in October 1809.

**Above and opposite page:** The Burggarten was laid out with the personal involvement of Emperor Franz I, who in Habsburg tradition had learned a trade and was a gardening enthusiast. The secessionist Palm House, built in 1901 by Friedrich Ohmann, is still used today; the centre part as a café-restaurant; the left wing houses the Butterfly House.

**Above right:** From 1848 under Emperor Franz Joseph the Burggarten was enlarged and redeveloped into an English landscape garden. The monument to the ruler is by Johannes Benk.
**Below right:** The Wolfgang Amadeus Mozart monument by Viktor Tilgner used to be on the Albertinaplatz and was moved to the Burggarten in 1953.

# JOSEFSPLATZ

Josefsplatz is characterised by the Austrian National Library, the former court library. Next to it is the Redoutensaal, which is named after its former function as a ballroom in which *Redouten* – fancy dress parties – were held. In the centre of the square is a monument to Emperor Joseph II by Franz Anton Zauner, which is a reminder of the great reform emperor. The oldest building on the square is the Augustinerkirche (St. Augustine's Church), which was hidden behind a Baroque façade in the 18th century to give the square a unified character. Today the handwriting collection of the national library can be found here.

**Opposite page and above:** The bronze rider's monument of Emperor Joseph II was built between 1795 and 1807 by Franz Anton Zauner. It is modelled on the statue of Marc Aurel on Capitoline Hill in Rome. It was commissioned by Emperor Franz II/I, who, from the age of 16, had been raised under the supervision of his Uncle Joseph II at the Viennese court.

**Below:** Josefsplatz, looking at the National Library and the Augustinerkirche façade.

# AUGUSTINERKIRCHE

The inscription on the tomb by Antonio Canova for Maria Theresia's daughter, Archduchess Marie Christine, Duke Albert of Saxony's wife, who installed a monument to his *uxori optimae* – "best wife" – in the Augustinerkirche. In the open gate is the allegorical figure of virtue with the urn accompanied by two girls carrying lit torches. They are followed by Caritas – love – leading a blind old man.

Even today, the entrance to the former Hofpfarrkirche dating back to the 14th century is through an inconspicuous gate on Josefsplatz. The church, consecrated in 1349, is the oldest maintained three-nave church from the mendicant order in Vienna. Its Baroque interior, which dates back to the 17th century, was restored in Gothic style by court architect Johann Ferdinand Hetzendorf von Hohenberg from 1784. Adjoining the choir is the two-nave Georgskapelle. St. George's knighthood, founded in the mid 14th century by Duke Otto the Merry, used to meet here. During the Baroque period the chapel became a charnel house, where the tomb of Emperor Leopold II can be found. After its elevation to a parish church of the imperial church in 1634, the Augustinerkirche (St. Augustine's Church) became the venue for the royal family's religious ceremonies – mainly weddings. This is where not only Maria Theresia and Franz Stephan of Lorraine were married, but also Emperor Franz Joseph and the Bavarian princess Elisabeth in 1854. However, the weddings were tightly closed affairs only taking place to the exclusion of the public and in front of dignitaries from the court.

For Franz Joseph's wedding to Elisabeth, family members met in the state rooms of the Leopoldine Wing, moving directly into the church, which was lit with 15,000 candles, through a passageway. The ceremony was held by Prince-Archbishop and Cardinal-to-be Othmar Rauscher, whose preaching was so excessive that he was given the nickname "Cardinal Plauscher" (a word meaning 'to chin-wag').

A distinctive feature of the church is the *Herzgrüftl*, where the hearts of the Habsburgs are kept in 54 urns. The church's most important monument is the tomb of Maria Theresia's favorite daughter, Archduchess Marie Christine, who died in 1798. Her husband, Duke Albrecht von Saxony-Teschen, founder of the Albertina, commissioned the Italian sculptor Antonio Canova to build the monument. He was also present at the opening in 1805.

View of the Hofburg from 1760 showing the yet unobstructed Augustinerkirche. In the centre is the National Library, on the right the Winter Riding School and on the far left the Albertina, Duke Albert of Saxony's palace.

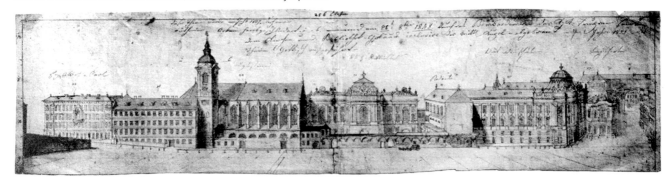

# A LOVE-MATCH IN THE HOUSE OF HABSBURG

Mimi, as Archduchess Marie Christina was called by her family, was the declared favourite daughter of Maria Theresia and the only one who was allowed to marry for love. Because daughters – in addition, Austrian archduchesses – were pawns of European politics in those times, and marriage contracts were only entered into for political reasons, this love-match represented a huge exception to the rule. First of all, however, the royal father Franz Stephan had to be convinced – he had already found a husband for Mimi. Maria Theresia gave her desperate daughter the following advice: *"Should this affair be successful, it must remain strictly secret. Above all you can never give him hope, never confide in anyone, for in any case the whole world pities you. I know your difficult situation and it aggrieves me. But only exercised restraint will lead to the desired goal. As your friend and mother I swear to reassure you and to put everything in God's hands – only with Him will you find peace [...] Show peace and courage to play the role that your duty demands of you. You are talented enough if only your will supports you with it. No small confidentiality or whispers in passing, neither with your sister or with anybody. Your happiness is what I desire for you, and in order to achieve it, I promise you that I will do everything in my power."*

It wasn't until after the sudden death of the emperor that Marie Christina was able to realise her dream and marry Duke Albert of Saxony in 1766. But in 1798 at the age of 56 the archduchess died from drinking contaminated water, upon which her husband Albert then had Vienna's first water system built. It was named after him.

Archduchess Marie-Christine of Saxony-Teschen.

Emperor Franz Joseph and the Bavarian Princess Elisabeth in Bavaria were married in the Augustinerkirche on 24 April 1854.

Grieving Genius with lion and the Saxony-Teschen coat of arms at the tomb by Canova.

According to the burial traditions of the imperial house the deceased were entombed in the Kapuzinergruft (Capuchin's Crypt). Their entrails lie in St Stephen's Cathedral and their hearts are kept in silver urns in the "Herzgrüftl" in the Augustinerkirche.

# COURT LIBRARY

Josefsplatz itself is characterised by the Austrian National Library, the former court library. Johann Bernhard and his son Joseph Emanuel Fischer von Erlach brought this main work of European Baroque architecture to fruition between 1721 and 1735. Originally free-standing from the Hofburg ensemble, the library was first connected to the Hofburg in the 1760s. The figures on the parapet are by Lorenzo Matielli and impressively present the goddess Pallas Athena in the centre. She is descending into ignorance and envy in her quadriga. Left is Atlas with the celestial globe and the allegories of Astronomy and Astrology, the sciences ascribed to him; on the right, Gaia, goddess of the earth with the allegories of Geometry and Geology.

The central domed hall, stretching over two floors is a grandiose *gesamtkunstwerk* and is one of the most beautiful library rooms in the world. The frescoes by Daniel Gran; the sculpture embellishments, the bookshelves and even the book covers are harmoniously coordinated with each other. The patron Charles VI is just as exalted in the ceiling painting as in the monument that shows him as "Hercules of the Muses" in the middle of the room.

The emperor did not only want the library – which around 1780 already had hundreds of thousands of objects – to be used privately, and from the beginning had made it accessible to scholars. Up to 40 of them at a time were allowed to work in the reading room, where they were even supplied with writing ink. The Prunksaal itself contains 200,000 volumes, the core of which is the precious library of Prince Eugene, the "Eugeniana".

The Austrian National Library's inventory encompasses about eight million objects, which, alongside the collection of printed materials that has about 2.8 million books, is divided up into the following categories: the Script and Incunabula collection, the Map Collection and Globe Museum, the Austrian literature archive, the music, papyrus, theatre and portrait collections and the picture archive.

**Opposite page:** Statue of Emperor Charles VI, the patron of the court library.
**Following double page:** Architecture, painting and décor unite in a Baroque *gesamtkunstwerk* in the Prunksaal of the National Library.
**Below:** The imperial court library. Etching by Carl Schütz and Johann Ziegler.

## THE BAROQUE COURT ARCHITECTS

Johann Bernhard Fischer von Erlach (1656 1723) was the first great architect of the Austrian Baroque. His main works in Vienna include the imperial summer residence Schloss Schönbrunn, Karlskirche (St. Charles' Church), the winter palace of Prince Eugene and Palais Lobkowitz, which today houses the Theatermuseum. From 1689 the architect tutored the emperor-to-be Joseph I in architecture; following the emperor's accession to power, Fischer von Erlach became Supervisor of Imperial Buildings. As an architect, his son Joseph Emanuel Fischer von Erlach (1693–1742) not only completed some of his father's unfinished projects, including the court library, but also built the Winter Riding School.

**Above:** To create an overall harmonious impression, the 15,000 books of Prince Eugene's precious library, which is situated in the centre oval, were uniformly bound.

**Opposite page:** The ceiling painting in the Augustine reading room of the National Library by Johann Wenzel Bergel dates back to 1772/73 and shows Parnassus and the allegories of the four faculties. A few years earlier, Bergel had so impressed Maria Theresia with his illusionist landscape paintings that she had him design the entire ground floor of her imperial summer residence in Schönbrunn Palace.

# REDOUTENSÄLE
# (REDOUBT HALLS)

The library was not the only Baroque construction project in the Hofburg. During Maria Theresia's reign between 1744 and 1748 the Redoutensäle were built in the place of an older opera and concert hall. The Redoutensäle were used for the imperial house's glittering festivities, but above all for colourful fancy-dress balls. Characteristic of the Habsburg's Baroque buildings were the multifunctional rooms that could be used as ballrooms.

Maria Theresia in particular loved theatre, the opera and glittering parties. She also encouraged family performances and had the most important contemporary musicians and poets study small operas and ballets with her children to perform them at birthdays or name days within the court circles. And it was not only the enjoyment of such events that was important, but Maria Theresia was also following a major pedagogical goal in having her children learn how to perform in public through the performances.

One of the highlights in the history of the Redoutensäle

**Above:** On the occasion of the wedding of Joseph II and Isabella of Parma in 1760 a magnificent supper was held in the Redoutensäle.
**Opposite page:** In contrast to the ball at court to which only high nobility was invited, 3,000 people annually attended the court ball in the Redoutensäle. Watercolour by Wilhelm Gause, ca. 1906.

were the magnificent wedding festivities connected to the wedding of the oldest son and successor to Maria Theresia, Joseph (II), to the Italian Princess Isabella of Parma. A few years later, Ludwig van Beethoven conducted in the venue, and shortly thereafter Franz Schubert conducted the premiere performances of Beethoven's Ninth and his own Unfinished Symphony; Johann Strauss son performed acclaimed waltz concerts here.

In 1992 a large fire caused major damage to the Redoutensaal Wing, which had been used as a congress centre for decades. Reconstruction followed between 1993 and 1997; the smaller Redoutensaal hadn't been as badly damaged and was able to be both historically and authentically reconstructed. The large Redoutensaal, however, was newly designed and painted with frescoes by Josef Mikl.

# STALLBURG

The residence for Maximilian II, begun in 1559, was soon remodelled into the Neue Stallung, namely in 1565 after it had been completed. Since then, it has housed the stables of the Lipizzaner horses. The Stallburg (mews) is one of Vienna's few Renaissance structures. Its external façades have kept their strict structure up to this day, although the side entrance lost its façade effect due to the flying buttresses that connect it to the Winter Riding School; the inner courtyard is arranged in rows of arcades.

**Right:** Every day, shortly before 10 a.m. the Lipizzans are led from their stables to training in the Winter Riding School.
**Below:** The stables of the Lipizzan horses have been located in the Stallburg since 1565.

# THE LIPIZZANS

The Spanish Riding School is the only institution in the world that maintains and cultivates the classic art of riding of the *haute école* from the Renaissance period. The only change has been the acceptance of women riders since 2008 – which, however, is not entirely new in the 430-year-old history of the riding school. Even during Maria Theresia's era, aristocratic girls were taught the *haute école* style. The horses received their name from their original stud Lipica in Slovenia. Today the Lipizzans are bred in the federal stud farm Piber in Styria and are sent to Vienna at the age of three-and-a-half for training.

Visitors can attend the gala performances as well as the so-called morning training sessions, which take place during the week. This daily training at the Winter Riding School provides insight into how the riders work with their horses.

The young stallions are trained for at least five years. Each horse has its own trainer-instructor who performs with the horse as well as takes responsibility for the horse's schooling.

**Right:** The Lipizzan stud farm is now in Piber, Styria.
**Below:** In 2008 the Stallburg underwent extensive refurbishment and the ground floor arcades were closed; the Lipizzans got a "room with a view".

The stables of the Lipizzans in the Stallburg.

**Left and right:** In the tack room the saddles and the artistically modelled tack are stored.

# WINTER RIDING SCHOOL

Opposite the Stallburg is the Winter Riding School, built by Josef Emanuel Fischer von Erlach between 1729 and 1735. It was built in place of the old "Paradeisgartl", the royal family's private garden.

The façade is characterised by a high base construction and divided by double columns that rise upwards to rounded columns that are crowned by a dome. The famous riding school hall, which takes up the entire interior of the building, forms a bright, austere and clearly structured space with a high base construction above which the main floor opens up in galleries. The Winter Riding School, which has been the home of the Spanish Riding School since Emperor Charles VI, was not used as a riding school but as a ball-room. This is where, in 1743, the famous ladies' carousel led by Maria Theresia took place when Prague was recaptured during the Austrian War of Succession. Court painter Martin van Meytens eternalized the event in a painting that is now hanging in Schönbrunn. The hall was also used for wedding celebrations and concerts. The first Austrian parliament session was actually held here on 14 March 1848 when the first peoples' assembly was taking place. From 22 July it was also the venue for the "constituent Reichstag", which was opened by Archduke Johann, a brother of Franz I. These days the famous gala performances are given here as well as the daily training sessions of the Spanish Riding School.

The performances of the Lipizzans in the Winter Riding School take place on the weekends. During the week they can be observed at training. As part of the gala performances the spectators experience the art of the *haute école* – the precision of the Lipizzans' movements to the music. The riders' uniform has remained unchanged for over 200 years and consists of a bi-corner black felt hat with a narrow or broad gold lining that indicates rank, brown uniform tails with a sewn-in pocket for sugar, deerskin breeches, knee-high boots, spurs and white deerskin gloves. The crop is made of birch and is custom-made by each rider.

**Right:** In the middle of the 19th century behind the Winter Riding School on Michaelerplatz was the old Hofburg theatre. It was not until 1888 that the theatre was torn down to make room for the Michaelertrakt. The new Burgtheater was built on the Ringstrasse.

**Below:** In December 1742, during the Austrian War of Succession when Bohemia was being rid of enemy troops, Maria Theresia held a Ladies' Carousel in the Winter Riding School. Also taking part in it herself, Maria Theresia and the ladies of the court danced a quadrille with horse and carriage and also competed in contests of skill.

# ZEREMONIENSAAL

Opposite the Heldenplatz is a building completed between 1802 and 1806 by Louis Montoyer; it houses the Zeremoniensaal (Ceremony Hall). This extension, found by contemporaries to be unharmonious, received the moniker 'Nose' due to its protruding position. In front of it in 1898 a connecting building to the Neue Burg with a winter garden and ballrooms was built.

The Zeremoniensaal was the venue for splendid parties and court balls, gala dinners and banquets. Only the high nobility, ministers, diplomats and the highest dignitaries were invited to the magnificent court balls. During Emporer Franz Joseph's reign the "Waltz King" and court kapellmeister Johann Strauss son conducted numerous court balls here. The highlight of the evening was the cotillion during which the men presented flower bouquets to their dance partners whose dance cards they had previously signed. Various dance figures brought young women and men together who wouldn't normally have danced with each other, giving them the opportunity to get make each others' acquaintance.

The second-biggest ball at court was the exclusive "Ball bei Hof" (court ball), which was reserved for members of the Habsburg family and one select part of the high nobility. Since 1958 the former ballrooms of the Habsburgs have been used for conferences and balls. A fixed part of carnival in Vienna even today, balls are seen as dancing events but are also used for hob-knobbing with old friends or networking in a festive atmosphere.

**Below:** Banquet in the Zeremoniensaal, lithography by Peter Geiger after Rudolf von Alt.

# NEUE BURG

The area around the Heldenplatz to the former court stables was originally planned as the Imperial Forum. It was supposed to document both the imperial standards of the House of Habsburg as well as the supranational identity of the multinational state. Late antique imperial palaces, St Peter's Square in Rome and above all the Zwinger in Dresden were the lavish models. This is why Gottfried Semper was called to Vienna. Together with the Viennese architect Carl Hasenauer, Semper planned the extensive project. Although construction began in the year 1879, only a small part was realised – the Corps de Logis near the Ring, which was going to be a guest wing, and the Neue Burg (New Hofburg Palace), which was completed by Ludwig Baumann.

The colonnade-like structure with its huge steady state front was originally planned as the residence of heir to the throne Franz Ferdinand. It wasn't built until shortly before the outbreak of World War I in 1913, which is also why the complex was never completed.

The completion of the interior didn't actually take place until after the fall of the monarchy between 1920 and 1926. Between the basement windows are 20 large sculptures that present the main epochs and bearers of Austria's history: a Marcomanni, a Roman legionary, a Bavarian, a missionary, a Slav, a Franconian count, a Magyars, a crusader, a mariner, a knight, a graduate, a merchant, a citizen, a miner, a lansquenet, a Wallenstein soldier, a Polish and Viennese citizen from the year of the second Turkish occupation 1683, a free farmer and finally a Tyrolean freedom fighter from 1809. Today the Neue Burg houses parts of the National Library, whose main reading room is on the ground floor, as well as collections from the Kunsthistorisches Museum.

**Above:** View through the Burgtor to the Neue Hofburg.
**Below:** The so-called "Hunting Plateau" in the Neue Burg.
**Following double page:** The curved colonnade front of the Neue Burg is the most representative façade of the Hofburg complex.

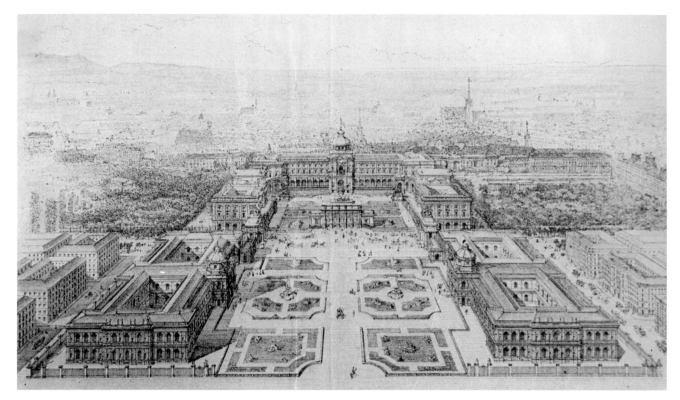

A domed throne hall was intended as the centre of the planned Imperial Forum. From its wings, semi-circular colonnades were to have surrounded Heldenplatz.

Since 1895 Austrian archaeologists have been excavating the ruins of Ephesos in Turkey, the most important Greek city and the then metropolis of the Roman province Asia. Numerous important findings have been exhibited in the Ephesos Museum in the Neue Burg since 1978, among other things, 40 metres of the 70 metre-long Parther frieze from the 2nd century AD.

**Above left:** The gala armour from 1578 is thought to come from the Archduke Ferdinand of Tyrol.

**Above right:** The Viennese collection is the best documented court armoury of the Western world because it consistently has objects that are connected to important political events – campaigns, legislative assemblies, coronations, engagements, weddings or christenings. All exhibited pieces of armour are individually crafted by the most famous armourers. Designs by famous artists such as Dürer and Holbein were often used for the armour's magnificent etchings.

**Right:** The collection of ancient music instruments in the Neue Burg is the world's most important collection of historical Renaissance music instruments. On display however are not only precious instruments that were played by the likes of Beethoven and Chopin but also the zither that Anton Karas used to play the melody to the film classic "The Third Man". An acoustic highlight of the collection is the only existing original recording of the Johann Strauss Kapelle.

The centre wing of the impressive Neue Hofburg complex is crowned by the imperial eagle and the Austrian imperial crown. On the balcony over the entrance, Adolf Hitler announced Austria's annexation to the German Empire in March 1938.

# HELDENPLATZ

Designing of the Heldenplatz (Heroes' Square) began with the withdrawal of Napoleon's troops in 1809 after they had blasted parts of the city wall that bordered the Hofburg, including the old city gate. A square then evolved between the imperial residence and the bourgeois Ringstrasse, which was built for the staging of political-symbolic productions. On the eastern side of the square in front of the Neue Burg the monument of Prince Eugene of Savoy, the "noble knight" was built. The bronze equestrian statue on a base made of Untersberg marble presents the commanders of three emperors Leopold I, Joseph I and Charles VI. The commission went to Anton Dominik Fernkorn in 1860. Fernkorn had previously created the monument of Archduke Charles, the victor over Napoleon in the battle of Aspern in 1809, which stands opposite the Prince Eugene statue. With this monument, Fernkorn managed a particularly successful feat, balancing the figure so that the rising horse is standing on its back legs and not, as usual, being supported by its tail.

**Right:** The monument to Prince Eugene of Savoy, who died in 1736, the "wise adviser of three emperors" and Austrian war hero, was commissioned in 1860 from the sculptor Anton Dominik Ritter von Fernkorn of Erfurt.

# The Hofburg complex

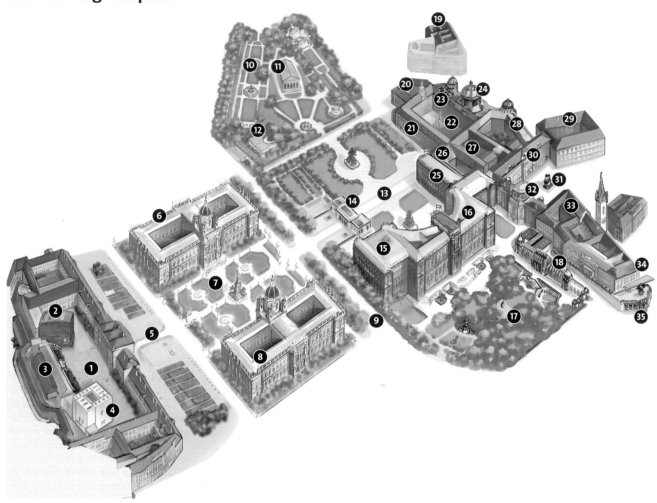

1  MuseumsQuartier
2  Museum of Modern Art
3  Kunsthalle Wien
4  Leopold Museum
5  Museumsplatz
6  Natural History Museum
7  Maria Theresien Platz
8  Art History Museum
9  Ringstrasse
10 Volksgarten
11 Theseus Temple
12 Volksgarten
13 Heldenplatz (Heroes' Square)
14 Burgtor
15 Corps de Logis
16 New Hofburg Palace
17 Burggarten
18 Palm House

19 Federal Chancellery
20 Amalienburg
21 Leopoldine Wing
22 In der Burg
23 Imperial Chancellery Wing
24 St Michael's Wing
25 State Halls Wing
26 Ceremony Hall
27 Swiss Court
28 Spanish Riding School
29 Stallburg
30 Redoutensaal Wing
31 Josefsplatz
32 Austrian National Library
33 St. Augustine's Church
34 Albertina
35 Danubius Fountain

# The bel étage apartments of the Hofburg in the 19th century

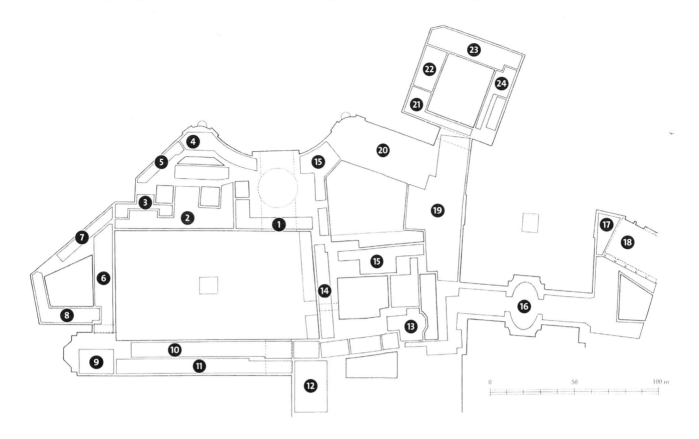

1  Apartment of Archduke Stephen, Palatine of Hungary; today the Sisi Museum
2  Emperor Franz Joseph's apartment
3  The offices of the emperor's *valet de chambre*
4  New guest apartments
5  The dwellings of Baron Franz Nopcsa, Empress Elisabeth's Lord Steward
6  Empress Elisabeth's apartment
7  The empress' chambers
8  The apartment of Tsar Alexander of Russia; used for court dinners during Emperor Franz Joseph's reign
9  St. Joseph's Chapel
10 Ceremony apartment, formerly the apartment of Empress Maria Theresia; today part of the Federal Chancellery
11 Large guest apartment; today part of the Federal Chancellery

12 Ceremony Hall
13 Hofburgkapelle
14 Field Marshal Radetzky's apartment
15 Guest apartment
16 Court Library
17 Zoological Court Cabinet
18 St. Augustine's Church
19 Redoutensäle (Redoubt Halls)
20 Winter Riding School
21 Apartment of the emperor's Lord Steward, Count Grünne
22 Apartment of the director of the court pharmacy
23 Apartment of the emperor's General Adjutant, Count de Crenneville
24 General manager of the court theatre

## Photo credits

Imagno/Austrian Archives: 31 (above), 35, 36 (below), 53, 66 (above and below), 69, 75, 81 (below)
Imagno/ÖNB: 26, 39 (left), 50 (below), 65 (below), 82, 86 (above)
Wien Museum: 74
Schönbrunn Betriebsgesellschaft m. b. H.: 25 (below)
Michael Appelt/Fotoagentur Anzenberger: 49 (above right)
Katrin Unterreiner collection: 24 (below), 34 (above and below), 50 (below), 81 (above)
T. Trenkler, Die Hofburg Wien. *Geschichte – Gebäude – Sehenswürdigkeiten* © Verlag Carl Ueberreuter GmbH, Wien 2004: 94
All other photos are originals by Willfried Gredler-Oxenbauer


The photographer would like to thank the following people for their support regarding the photos:
Ilse Jung and team (Art History Museum, Treasury, Hofburg Armoury, Ancient Music collection, Ephesos Museum)
Mag. Doris Becker (Austrian National Library, Prunksaal, Augustiner reading room, reading rooms, Globe Museum, Papyrus Museum)
P. Albin Scheuch OSA and Ursula Lechner (Augustinerkirche)
Petra Reichetzer and team (Spanish Riding School)
Mag. Michaela Gold and Harald Gruber (Silberkammer, Sisi Museum and Imperial Apartments)

The author would like to thank chief palace administrator Hofrat Wolfgang Beer for the friendly tour of the Hofburg

## Die Autorin

**Katrin Unterreiner** – until 2007 scientific director of the Imperial Apartments of the Vienna Hofburg and curator of the Sisi Museum. Numerous exhibitions (including the "Crown Prince Rudolf" exhibition) as well as publications on the Vienna Hofburg and the daily culture of the Viennese court.

## Der Fotograf

**Willfried Gredler-Oxenbauer**, freelancer for various media and publishing houses in Austria. His main focus is the coverage and documentation of nature, architecture and people.

ISBN 978-3-85431-491-2

© 2009 by Pichler Verlag in der Verlagsgruppe Styria GmbH & Co KG
Vienna-Graz-Klagenfurt
All rights reserved
www.pichlerverlag.at

Cover design: Bruno Wegscheider
Graphics and layout: Franz Hanns
Translation: Mý Huê McGowran

Reproduction: Pixelstorm, Vienna
Printing and binding: Druckerei Theiss GmbH, St. Stefan im Lavanttal